OFF

The Day the Internet Died
A Bedtime Fantasy

WRITTEN BY CHRIS COLIN
ILLUSTRATED BY RINEE SHAH

PRESTEL
MUNICH · LONDON · NEW YORK

On the day the screens went dark,
I stood in the yard and the sun shone brightly
but I was brought low for I knew not where the
stars of "Saved by the Bell" were now, nor
which remained hot, and the information
could not be Googled thereof.

You
HAD ME
AT TACOS

On the day the screens went dark,
mine laptop bore no invitation to purchase
printer ink nor CBD oil; nor did Aunt Kim
linketh to broken religious websites.

COME UNTO ME, CHILDREN,

I declared, LET US WALK, IRL.

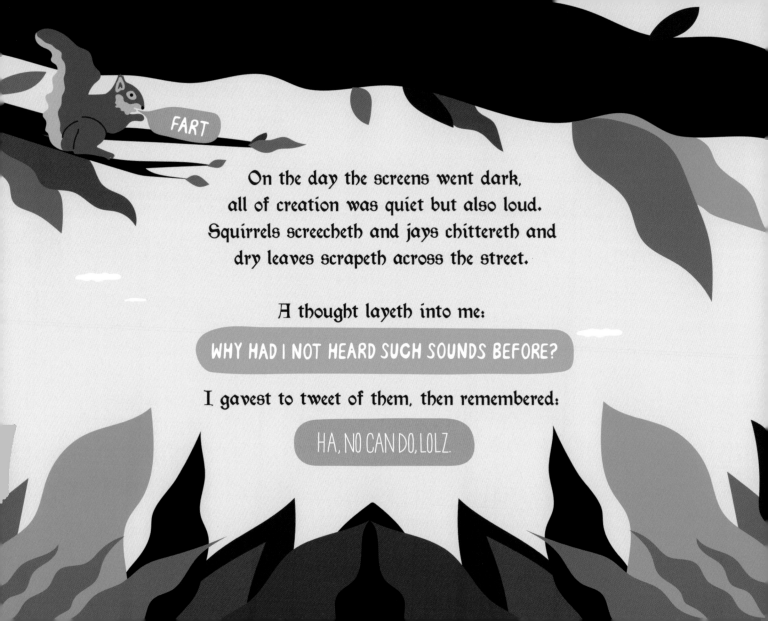

FART

On the day the screens went dark,
all of creation was quiet but also loud.
Squirrels screecheth and jays chittereth and
dry leaves scrapeth across the street.

A thought layeth into me:

WHY HAD I NOT HEARD SUCH SOUNDS BEFORE?

I gavest to tweet of them, then remembered:

HA, NO CAN DO, LOLZ.

On the day the screens went dark,
33,298 New Yorkers refreshed no news feeds,
21,983 Parisians knew not how long their commutes would take,
and 7,332 Londoners listened to an unfamiliar podcast
consisting of . . . their thoughts.

LET ME &^$% PERISH,

all saidst unto themselves, though some also
felt a strange calm.

WHAT SWEET NEW CALMING APP HATH INSTALLED

they wondered. But there was none.

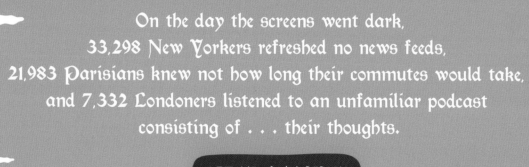

We toiled and toiled, then beheld what we'd wrought. It would receive neither fave nor heart, nor Aunt Kim's supplemental conspiracy links.

But we ate of it with vigor.

On the day the screens went dark,
I swiped neither left nor right upon
the toilet, nor angered any birds.
In and out in three minutes.

On the day the screens went dark,
I took mine old flute down from the closet,
and gazed upon a cloud that resembled a
camel and played fourteenfold rounds of
Go Fish with the children
— a plague upon them both!

But still there was time for reflection.
I reflected on the ceiling, and imagined walking
up there, how clean and bare it was,
a thought unvisited for years.

On the day the screens went dark,
threescore inches of sewage streamed unto the basement
because forsooth, turns out the Internet controls the
something something wastewater treatment sensor something.
Okay, so, mixed bag.

On the day the screens went dark,
change swept over hearth and home, and over sea
and sky, and over a couple at the Burger Bling
down the street.

HERE IS EVERY DETAIL FROM MY MEETING WITH VICKI FROM HR,

spake the woman, and lo there were many,
but the man turned not once to his phone.

O, YE ARE SUPER PRESENT AND IT PLEASETH!

saidth the woman.

On the morrow they ate of the 𝔚hopper again,
and in twelve moons' time they welcomed
a babe into their arms, and exclaimed,

HELLO TEESVONDRUH!

for they'd now also had time to
get way into D&D.

In the year the screens went dark,
our children lay upon grass, and rode
upon horses, and trembled at rainbows, for feeling
now suffused their hearts where once
distraction dwelleth.

LET US PLAY MINECRAFT FOR NINE FREAKING HOURS,

they would say, and it would come to pass,
for Minecraft was a game involving sticks
and leaves.

Food was better and music richer, shuttered IT departments made art from USB cables and dew drops, and Aunt Kim traded her laptop for Bhangra classes.

Many felt peaceful and some felt lonely. A farmer in Laos would never fall in love in his favorite turnip chat room, for turnip chat rooms ceased.

BUT IT WAS GOOD,

the people said.

They were alive, and it was holy
to be awake, and their saga liveth in the book
you now holdeth, four out of four hearts,
seven billion actual thumbs up.

Prestel Verlag, Munich · London · New York 2021
A member of Verlagsgruppe Random House GmbH
Neumarkter Strasse 28 · 81673 Munich

Library of Congress Cataloging-in-Publication Data
Names: Colin, Chris, 1975- author. | Shah, Rinee, illustrator.
Title: Off : the day the Internet died : a bedtime fantasy / written by
Chris Colin ; illustrated by Rinee Shah.
Description: Munich ; New York : Prestel, [2021]
Identifiers: LCCN 2020010926 | ISBN 9783791386874 (hardcover)
Subjects: LCSH: Internet--Social aspects--Humor. | Social media--Humor.
Classification: LCC PN6231.I62 C65 2021 | DDC 818/.602--dc23
LC record available at https://lccn.loc.gov/2020010926

A CIP catalogue record for this book is available from
the British Library.

Editorial direction: Holly La Due
Design & Production: Anjali Pala
Copyediting: John Son

Verlagsgruppe Random House FSC® N001967
Printed on the FSC®-certified paper

Printed in China
ISBN 978-3-7913-8687-4

www.prestel.com